James Whateley and the Survival of Chartism

Stephen Roberts

Published under the imprint *Birmingham Biographies*

Printed by CreateSpace

ISBN-13: 978-1983503030

ISBN-10: 1983503037

Front cover: A Birmingham polling card – for a period James Whateley represented St. George's ward. With the exception of the three cartoons and the three photographs, which are reproduced by permission of, respectively, the Birmingham and Midland Institute and Douglas Wilks, all illustrations in this book are taken from the author's collection

To the memory of Theophilus Hall who 'drowned himself through fright during the Chartist riots'.

Contents

Acknowledgements

In researching and writing this book, I have been able to call on the support of a number of people. Richard Brown and Carl Chinn both read the text and assured me that I was on the right track. Sue Curtis provided genealogical information about my two subjects. Ewan Fernie proved to be a kind supporter of what I am doing (and have done). Jennifer Grey sent me a copy of her essay about the Birmingham Baptist the Revd. Thomas Swan. Les Rosenthal provided statistical information about James Whateley's voting record as a town councillor. Len Smith shared his knowledge of the Kidderminster Chartist George Holloway with me. Victoria Osborne took me to see the wonderful portrait of Arthur O'Neill, which is in storage at Birmingham Museum and Art Gallery. Douglas Wilks took the three photographs of Key Hill cemetery and gave permission for them to be reproduced in this book. Councillor Rob Pocock answered a query about the layout of the council house. Councillors John Cotton and Ian Ward invited me to the council house to discuss my work on Victorian Birmingham.

Much of the research for this book was done – as these things often are these days – in front of a computer screen at home and in easy reach of a cup of coffee. The British Newspaper Archive has been an invaluable source of information. Harris Manchester College, Oxford, provided me with copies of the obituaries for Charles Clarke. I am glad to say that I did manage to leave my study – and, once again, found the peace and help I needed in the library of the Birmingham and Midland Institute. The cartoons from the *Dart* which appear in this book are reproduced by permission of the BMI.

I. Who were the Birmingham Chartists?

irmingham was at the centre of the Chartist agitation for less a
year – yet the Chartist ideal survived in the town for half a
century. The reason for this was that the working class leaders of
the local movement continued to reside in the town in the ensuing
decades and persisted in behaving like Chartists. Arthur O'Neill,
the pastor of the Chartist Church and later of the Zion Baptist
Chapel, was the most important of these men. Frequently to be
found addressing public meetings in the town, he would remind
audiences of his former associations – he was, he declared at a
meeting of the National Old Age Pensions League in October
1894, 'the oldest living minister but one in Birmingham, the oldest
Chartist and the only living Chartist who had been in prison for
Chartism ...'[1] James Whateley, O'Neill's right-hand man at the
Chartist Church, was another stalwart who continued to advocate
the tenets of Chartism. When he was elected to the town council in
1871, he made clear that he was an advocate for the working class
and urged the removal of obstacles, such as the early closing of
polling stations, which hampered working class participation in
municipal elections. Long into the century the old cause was still
championed 'often at great sacrifice' by men who did not become
well-known local figures – such as John Rutherford and John Mills,
the latter identifying himself as a Chartist at a meeting for the
unemployed in January 1885.[2]

It was in Birmingham, in 1838-9, that the plans for the first
national petition and convention were launched and where the first
sustained clash between working people and the police and soldiers
took place. The petition was adopted at a meeting at Holloway
Head on Monday 6 August 1838. With Newhall Hill, the scene of
the famous open-air meeting of May 1832, now heavily built on, this
natural amphitheatre was selected by the recently-revived
Birmingham Political Union for its great demonstration. Working
people from across the midlands, with their bands and flags and led

---

[1] *Birmingham Daily Post*, 25 October 1894.
[2] *Birmingham Daily Gazette*, 23 April, 9 May 1867; *Birmingham Daily Post*, 16 January 1885.

1

by gun makers, brass founders, pin makers and other trades, marched the short distance from the town centre to the wasteland known as Holloway Head. This huge turnout of support was divided into 'divisions', or, as the main speaker Thomas Attwood put it in his speech, 'battalions'.[3] The speakers also included Feargus O'Connor and several other well-known radicals from the north and Scotland and they testified that they saw 'eight acres of men' – the crowd very probably reached 200,000.[4] At the beginning of the year the middle class leaders of the BPU had declared themselves in favour of a say in law-making for all adult men and women. Now Attwood, after requesting the removal of hats whilst he said a prayer, explained how a national petition and, if necessary, a 'sacred month' would bring an end to high food prices, the New Poor Law and the Corn Laws; the Tory-supporting *Aris' Gazette* chose not to report the speeches of the other speakers lest its readers took alarm but offered the reassurance that the event had been 'a total failure'.[5]

If the conversion of the heroes of the 1832 agitation to universal suffrage and the great demonstration at Holloway Head had appeared to suggest that middle class and working class reformers were united, ensuing developments revealed that it was the weakest of alliances. The leaders of the BPU and the working men's committee met on different evenings, and there was a dispute about how rent should be collected to support delegates to the Chartist convention. In March 1839, T.C. Salt, R.K. Douglas and the other middle class delegates elected at the Holloway Head meeting to represent the town resigned from the convention. Unlike during the Reform Bill agitation, they were not in control of the popular movement and did not find the class-infused language of the *Northern Star* at all to their taste. To their dismay the

---

[3] *Birmingham Journal*, 11 August 1838; *Aris's Birmingham Gazette*, 13 August 1838.

[4] *Birmingham Journal*, 11 August 1838.

[5] *Aris's Birmingham Gazette*, 13 August 1838. One of those who wasn't at all alarmed by O'Connor was Brooke Foss Westcott (1825-1901), who grew up in Birmingham and later became bishop of Durham: 'My father took the keenest interest in the Chartist Movement ... he deserted his meals to be present at various stirring meetings, in particular to listen to the oratory of "the great agitator"' (*Birmingham Daily Post*, 7 April 1903).

convention did not break up but re-located from London to Birmingham.

The rupture of the uneasy alliance of 1838 was brought to its conclusion with the riots in the Bull Ring.[6] Meetings to hear Chartist speeches in the Bull Ring had begun at the start of 1839. A Chartist eyewitness recalled that they 'were orderly ... and the shopkeepers and the market people can only say it was a nuisance to have hundreds of people in the way of their cabbage-selling and the cheering annoyed the Mrs Candles of that day who would persist in late evening shopping'.[7] However, as the meetings grew in frequency and strength, they were banned by the magistrates, a number of whom were leading figures in the now-dissolved BPU. With the arrival of sixty police officers from London in early July, with the intention of arresting the speakers, a series of confrontations broke out over the next fortnight, culminating on 15 July in a takeover of the streets by working people and the destruction of property. Subsequent meetings were immediately broken up by patrols by the police and the Fourth Irish Dragoons. The outcome of all this was that William Lovett and John Collins – both members of the convention - were imprisoned for producing a handbill condemning the actions of the authorities, another eleven were imprisoned with hard labour for riotous assembly and two were transported for property destruction.

The clashes between working people and the police and soldiers in summer 1839 lived long in the minds of the inhabitants of Birmingham. Neither the anti-Catholic Murphy riots of 1867 or the anti-Tory riots in Aston Park in 1884 evoked the same potency. Seventy years afterwards a local newspaper published a series of recollections of what had happened in 1839. There were stories that had been passed down in families. John Suffield, a draper, remembered one of his uncle's employees, out after the 8pm curfew, encountering 'a troop of cavalry and one of the soldiers swerved out of rank and made a cut at him with his drawn sword. He ducked his head but came home ... with a white, scared face

---

[6] C. Behagg, *Politics & Production in the Early Nineteenth Century* (1990), pp. 202-222.

[7] *Birmingham Daily Post*, 28 January 1939. For other centenary accounts of the Bull Ring riots see *Birmingham Daily Gazette*, 6 July, 14 July 1939 and *Birmingham Daily Mail*, 6 July 1939.

which had found itself too near cold steel to be pleasant'.[8] There were memories of the magistrates – of Robert Webb declaring himself unable to go out and read the Riot Act because 'the gout seized him suddenly – perhaps through fright' and of the magistrate David Nelson riding on horseback at the head of a squadron of cavalry.[9] There were vivid descriptions of the violence. 'The Chartists broke into shops in the Bull Ring and set the premises afire and boxes of tea were soon blazing in the road', Alfred Davenport recollected. 'The cavalry charged the rioters using the flats of their swords. The Chartists pulled down the railings and everything that offered for missiles and weapons of defence or offence'.[10] Another witness, who identified himself as 'Octogenarian', recalled that 'the cavalry tried to use the flats of their swords, but they had to use more severe measures. When the following morning, I went as far as Cherry Street, there was evidence of a fierce struggle having taken place between the rioters and the soldiery for blood was to be seen in the doorsteps where one or other had taken shelter.'[11] When it came to explaining the causes of the riots, these men were all of one mind: Chartist meetings should not have been prohibited and the London police should not have been brought in.

The events of summer were always known in Birmingham as 'the Chartist riots'. In later decades accusing their Liberal opponents of being Chartists became a favourite tactic of the Tories. For these politicians, Chartism had been 'that weary, miserable ... agitation ... (a) plague' and when the Liberal councillor Henry Hawkes called a Tory candidate 'the duck-legged drummer boy' he was immediately reminded of 'his notoriety ... in connection with the ... Chartist movement ... he found it very difficult to shake off his early impressions'. [12] Hawkes doubtless believed that he got the better of the exchange and, like his very good friends O'Neill and Whateley, remained proud of his Chartist connections.[13] So,

---

[8] *Birmingham Daily Gazette,* 27 March 1908. John Suffield was the grandfather of J.R.R. Tolkein.

[9] Ibid., 16 January 1908.

[10] Ibid.

[11] Ibid., 21 November 1907. Ibid., 15 May 1908 for the Chartist recollections of George Davies, replete with hostility towards O'Connor.

[12] *Aris's Birmingham Gazette,* 31 October 1868, 3 September 1877.

too, did Bertram Ladkin, who came forward as a Labour candidate in the city council elections in November 1911 and November 1912. He was very pleased to announce that he was the grandson of the Manchester Chartist W.H. Chadwick, who had died in 1908, and 'spoke at length of the necessity of having labour representation on the city council to protect the interests of the workers.'[14] It was good Chartist talk, but Ladkin was not to be elected.

Though the Chartists did disappear from the streets of Birmingham in the aftermath of the Bull Ring riots, they still continued to meet in chapels and coffee houses, principally to organise assistance for the men who were transported in 1839-40.[15] It was widely believed that Francis Roberts, convicted and transported on the evidence only of a police constable, had not been present at all in the Bull Ring on the evening that two shops were set alight; his wife was deemed 'a Whig-made widow'.[16] Separate committees existed for him, for John Collins, who was in Warwick Gaol, and for the leaders of the Newport Rising. In November 1840 twenty-nine men took out cards to join the National Charter Association, with another forty-two waiting for their cards; and an organising committee of seven was formed.[17] The arrival two months later of George White in the town as correspondent for the *Star* gave the local movement the bold leadership it needed. A West Riding Chartist who had already been imprisoned, White was fiercely class conscious, regarding middle class reformers as 'our most bitter and deadly enemies', ever

---

[13] Henry Hawkes (1813-91) was first elected to the town council in 1846. Like O'Neill and Whateley, he was an advocate of peace and international arbitration. For the last sixteen years of his life he served as the coroner for Birmingham.

[14] *Birmingham Daily Gazette,* 17 September 1912. Ladkin had served as a soldier in South Africa, where he was twice wounded, and had also been an actor; he was at this time a salesman and secretary of the Birmingham Vanmen's Union. Sparkbrook, 1912: Stephenson (Liberal Unionist), 1322; Ray (Liberal), 915; Ladkin (Labour), 397.

[15] *Northern Star,* 9 November 1839 for a meeting of the Women's Political Union. Here see H. Rogers, *Women and the People: Authority, Authorship and the Radical Tradition in Nineteenth Century England* (Aldershot, 2000), pp. 85-101.

[16] *Northern Star,* 4 July, 17 October, 5 December 1840.

[17] Ibid., 21 November 1840.

ready to betray the people.[18] If O'Connor wanted to make Birmingham a Chartist stronghold, he had picked the right man. Feargus was welcomed to the Bull Ring by huge crowds in September 1841, 1,200 NCA cards were taken out and meetings of the Anti-Corn Law League and Complete Suffrage Union were stormed.

All of this was viewed with concern by another new arrival to the town. Arthur O'Neill was a Glasgow Chartist preacher who believed that arguments were won not by shows of numbers but by lectures and tracts. He was invited to take up residence in Birmingham as pastor of the newly-established Chartist Church by John Collins, who was released from prison in July 1840 and who kept out of the NCA. The Chartist Church in Newhall Street recruited 250-300 members, including a large number of young women.[19] These working people were deeply loyal to their pastor, embracing teetotalism and, in some cases, vegetarianism, entering his essay competitions and going out across the town with him with placards and handbills.

In Joseph Sturge O'Neill had a supporter who provided both encouragement and money. Sturge was a resident of Edgbaston, and the two men were in regular contact. In contrast his relationship with White was perpetually strained. He declared the NCA to be illegal and stayed away from the O'Connor demonstration; for his part, White denounced the Chartist Church as 'a parcel of fanatics and not Chartists or Christians'.[20] Irrespective of their differences, both men were arrested and imprisoned during the strikes of summer 1842. White had stirred memories of the Bull Ring riots by organising nightly meetings and processions in the town; he spent eight months in prison for his trouble. O'Neill informed a meeting of strikers that he would refuse to pay income tax; his reward was twelve months in prison.

---

[18] S. Roberts, *Radical Politicians and Poets in Early Victorian Britain: The Voices of Six Chartist Leaders* (New York, 1993), p. 20; ibid., pp. 17-21 for a full discussion of White's Birmingham years.

[19] Amongst these women was Sarah Oxford: see her interesting letter in the *Birmingham Journal*, 6 March 1841.

[20] S. Roberts *The Chartist Prisoners: The Radical Lives of Thomas Cooper (1805-1892) and Arthur O'Neill (1819-1896)* (Oxford), p. 65; ibid., pp. 62-8 for a full discussion of the Chartist Church.

The two men emerged from their prison cells in, respectively, January and August 1844. Though White was to return to Birmingham for several months in winter 1855-6 to lead protests against high bread prices, he spent most of the rest of his life in the West Riding. He died in Sheffield workhouse in June 1868, his wish for a final conversation with old friends denied because it wasn't visiting day.[21] O'Neill long outlived White. He settled in Birmingham, marrying a member of his congregation in June 1845 and, twelve months later, taking charge of the Zion Baptist Chapel, located directly opposite a canal wharf in Newhall Street. 'Birmingham without Mr O'Neill would never have been quite the same place ...', E. Lawley Parker, the mayor, observed half a century later.[22]

From the pulpit of Zion Baptist Chapel, O'Neil continued to preach the messages of political justice for working people, peace and temperance that his congregation at the Chartist Church – many of whom followed him to his new chapel – were familiar with. In 1851 his Sunday morning and evening congregations stood at an average of, respectively, 280 and 460, including children.[23] From this point on, however, the congregation steadily fell and by the early 1860s was raising the smallest sums of all the chapels in the town for the Baptist Missionary Society.[24] Nevertheless, such events as the summer peace service and the Christmas tea continued to be held.

O'Neill's congregation was primarily made up of the poor. A journalist who attended a service in May 1871 noted a congregation of about thirty and drew attention to young women who 'distinguished themselves by a display of unmistakeable

---

[21] *Reynolds' Newspaper,* 9 August 1868.

[22] *Birmingham Daily Post,* 13 August 1891. O'Neill was baptised by Thomas Swan, the leading Baptist minister in the town, in June 1846. I am grateful to Jennifer Gray for letting me read a revised version of her essay on Swan, which was first published in the *Birmingham Historian,* no. 31 (2007).

[23] K. Geary, ed. *The 1851 Census of Religious Worship: Church, Chapel and Meeting Place in Mid-Nineteenth Century Warwickshire* (Stratford-upon-Avon, 2014), p. 119.

[24] *Birmingham Daily Gazette,* 16 May 1861, 22 May 1862. In 1861 O'Neill's congregation raised £5. 6s in contrast to the £85. 5s. 10d raised by the Cannon Street Chapel.

"Brummagem" jewellery, particularly in the matter of earrings, some of which were as large as crown pieces ... (and which) scarcely harmonized with stuff gowns and shawls which had seen better days.'[25] According to this report O'Neill's chapel was 'a sorry, shabby, neglected-looking place, devoid of beauty, taste and comfort.'[26] 'It is a long time since we have had our tympanum so seriously disarranged', he tartly commented of the choir.[27] O'Neill, he decided, 'doesn't ape humility; we even doubt whether he possesses it in any considerable degree'; but he had a 'commanding presence' and 'a fine, powerful voice' and 'his sermons are well worth hearing ... thoroughly interesting – rather narrative in character than doctrinal ... eminently a picturesque preacher.'[28] And he recognised something else in the O'Neill: this was an old Chartist speaking.

W.H. Day was an admirer of Arthur O'Neill and a life-long friend of James Whateley. At first he worked as a pearl button maker, but then secured employment with the Post Office. He was a member of the congregation of O'Neill's Chartist Church and subsequently of the congregation at the Zion Baptist Chapel. He stayed loyal to his pastor for decades, serving at different times as a trustee, treasurer and secretary of the chapel. He declared that he had 'during that time imbibed the principles of the People's Charter as advocated by Mr O'Neill and he had no doubt he should carry those principles to his grave'.[29]

---

[25] *Birmingham Daily Mail*, 8 May 1871.

[26] Ibid.

[27] Ibid.

[28] Ibid. *Birmingham Daily Mail*, 11 September 1915, where O'Neill is remembered as 'a delightful old man'.

[29] *Birmingham Daily Post*, 30 December 1885. Shortly afterwards O'Neill retired as pastor. His successor lasted just twelve months and thereafter services were taken by members of the congregation. As the congregation dwindled, the Sunday morning service was abandoned. The residents of the adjacent burial ground were re-interred in Witton cemetery in April 1903 by which time the chapel was serving as a mission room for St. Martin's Church (*Birmingham Daily Gazette,* 27 April 1903).

II. The Chartist Councillor: James Whateley (1823-1893)

I A Chartist Reunion

For the Revd. Arthur O'Neill, minister of the Zion Baptist Chapel in Newhall Street, Birmingham, the afternoon of Monday 23 November 1885 would be memorable and humbling. That afternoon O'Neill addressed a meeting at the town hall, as he had, over the decades, done many times before. This time, however, it was not just another routine political meeting. With admission free, a 'vast crowd' assembled to witness the presentation of an illuminated address to O'Neill and the unveiling of his portrait, commissioned by 'a numerous body of subscribers' and painted by local artist Jonathan Pratt, for display in the 'Gallery of Birmingham Portraits' in the newly-opened Art Gallery.[1] With the exception of Joseph Chamberlain, the leading luminaries of Birmingham Liberalism were in attendance – J.T. Bunce, George Dixon, Francis Schnadhorst, Richard Tangye, Sam Timmins and John Bright, who was to deliver the tribute. It was forty-five years since O'Neill had arrived in Birmingham to take up the position of pastor at the Chartist Church in Newhall Street and the 'magnificent' – as he described it - Reform Act of 1884 had now seemed to have almost put into place the first demand of the People's Charter.[2] The meeting was intended to be a celebration of the life's work of this veteran radical. In November 1885 it seemed that the old Chartist had been right all along.

At least that's what it seemed to most of the audience, who greeted mentions of the Chartists with loud cheers. Over the course of an hour Bright declared himself to be largely in agreement with the six points of the People's Charter, but found it

---

[1] *Birmingham Daily Post,* 24 November 1885. Jonathan Pratt (1835-1911) had arrived in Birmingham from Lincoln in 1863. His painting 'Latest Intelligence', inspired by the Franco-Prussian war, was exhibited at the Royal Academy. He was also noted for painting scenes of local people in Brittany. According to the *Birmingham Daily Gazette,* 15 October 1932, the portrait of O'Neill could be found in a corridor of the Council House: it was put into storage after the Second World War.

[2] *Birmingham Daily Post,* 24 November 1885.

necessary to draw attention to demagogues who had 'made use of ... (the) suffering of the people' and who had 'us(ed) language of the most outrageous violence and menace' and who were under 'an excitement that approached a condition of madness'.[3] When challenged from the hall, he refused to identify these men, but it was clear to those who heard him that he was referring to Joseph Rayner Stephens and Feargus O'Connor.[4] When O'Neill occasionally offered interjections, Bright seemed to forget that this wasn't his afternoon. 'Now Mr O'Neill', he half-jocularly observed, 'you have had your time. Mr O'Neill has discussed these questions so long ago we cannot allow him to discuss them again.'[5] His speech delivered, Bright left; by evening he was back in Rochdale.

This was a Chartist reunion, of sorts. O'Neill was not the only former Chartist in the town hall on that afternoon. Also there was Charles Clarke, once a Chartist 'missionary' in the West of England and, for thirty years, Unitarian minister at the Old Meeting House in New Street. And, occupying the chair, was James Whateley, who, in the early 1840s, had been O'Neill's indispensable helper at the Chartist Church. In his opening remarks Whateley remembered the trials, imprisonments and transportations of the Chartist martyrs. 'It was very different then to advocate Liberal principles to what it is these days', he declared. 'It was dangerous then for almost anyone to open his mouth about political matters for men were apprehended and incarcerated ... Frost, Williams and Jones were tried and condemned to death because they advocated the People's Charter'.[6] Condemned to death for advocacy of the People's Charter? Bright would not have endorsed that remark. O'Neill addressed his friend as 'dear old brother Chartist Whateley', and sought to mollify Bright by describing how he had sought 'to bring the good, quiet, intelligent Chartists together and, like a bit of a parson as he was, he helped to bring religion into the matter as the basis of the rights of man.'[7]

---

[3] Ibid.

[4] The trade union leader Henry Broadhurst, who represented Bordesley in 1885-6, in fact identified Stephens at the end of the meeting, stating that there were 'many excuses' for his fiery language.

[5] *Birmingham Daily Post*, 24 November 1885.

[6] Ibid.

[7] Ibid. Six years later O'Neill was presented with an address and an album

The idea of paying a public tribute to O'Neill had been Whateley's. He had been stirred into action by reading the first of a series of recollections about early Chartism which O'Neill had contributed to a local morning newspaper.[8] In a letter to the newspaper in January 1885 headed 'The Charter and the Franchise Act' he recalled the 'excellent' demonstrations of the 1840s and called a meeting at local coffee house – a teetotaller, Whateley was a shareholder in the Birmingham Coffee House Company - for former members of the Chartist Church. 'I shall be glad to see them on an important matter', Whateley wrote.[9] And so a small group of former Chartists met at the coffee house in New Street at 8 p.m. on Saturday 24 January 1885. Unfortunately, no record of their names has survived, though one was probably A.J. Hutchinson. These men needed an influential and powerful ally, and Whateley found one. The Smethwick entrepreneur Richard Tangye agreed to serve as treasurer of a newly-established committee, set up to raise funds to commission the illuminated address and the portrait. By August the 'striking portrait' of O'Neill, clutching a copy of the People' Charter, had been completed and was on public display.[10]

James Whateley was the only former Chartist elected to the town council during the Chamberlain era. With him, the Chartist ideal survived. When he first came forward, it was, at his insistence, not as a Liberal but as a working man's candidate, and the need for working class representation on the town council and in Parliament were issues that he never stopped talking about. Whateley served as a councillor for twenty-two years, but, unlike other long-serving

---

of photographs in the council house to mark his fifty years in Birmingham. The meeting was chaired by Whateley and O'Neill reminisced about his earlier life: 'They were hanging people in rows. Daniel O'Connell once told him of eighteen men being hanged in a row; and there was reason to believe every one was innocent.' (Ibid., 13 August 1891).

[8] Ibid., 21 January ('The People's Charter and the Franchise Act'), 28 January ('The Main Causes of the Chartist Agitation'), 11 February ('Influence of Birmingham on the Chartist Movement') and 23 February 1885 ('The Chartist National Convention'); S. Roberts, *The Chartist Prisoners,* pp. 19-20.

[9] *Birmingham Daily Post,* 22 January 1885.

[10] Ibid., 25 August 1885.

councillors, the former Chartist was never appointed an alderman, let alone considered for mayor.

II 'I have roared for "No Property Qualification" with the best of the Birmingham Chartists ...'

James Whateley was not born in Birmingham, but he spent almost all his life in the town. He was the eldest son of George Whateley, born in Castle Bromwich in 1799 and later a chair maker and part-time police constable, and Elizabeth Hodgetts, who was born in Aston in 1801. He was born in Wyle Cop, Shrewsbury, on 6 April 1823, his four brothers and four sisters being born in Birmingham between 1825 and 1844.[11]   There was work for chair makers in Birmingham as well as family ties and that is where his parents settled soon after his birth. Whateley's obituary is silent about his early life, but we do know that, on 13 December 1846, at the age of twenty-three, he married Mary Rogers at St. Philip's Church. Living in Moland Street, he worked as a pearl button maker.

All sorts of buttons were made in Birmingham – buttons in metal, buttons in linen, buttons in horn, buttons in wood, buttons in glass. In the middle of the century it was estimated that the pearl button trade provided employment for about two thousand people, making use of over twenty tons of shells – sourced from South America and later Australia - each week.[12] Sorting and cutting the shells was done mainly by women and children. Turning and polishing these delicate items needed to be done carefully and was undertaken by skilled men, who worked by hand with the aid of a foot lathe. Whateley was employed by one of the largest button manufacturers in the town, Hammond, Turner & Sons of Snow Hill. Through Sir Robert Peel the firm presented Prince Albert with a selection of buttons in November 1843 and in June 1847 the former Prime Minister accompanied the Grand Duke of Russia

---

[11] Whateley's siblings were: George (b. 1825); John (b. 1827); Elizabeth (b. 1832); Alfred (b. 1834); Hannah (b. 1835); Charles (b. 1839); Eliza (b. 1841); Selina (b. 1844). Both Alfred and Charles worked as lapidaries, cutting and polishing gems.
[12] S. Timmins, ed. *The Resources, Products and Industrial History of Birmingham and the Midland Hardware District* (1866)

(one of a number of visiting dignitaries over the years) on a tour of the premises. [13]

William Hammond Turner, James Turner and Henry Turner joined the clamour for the repeal of the Corn Laws. Their fervour spread to their employees, forty-three of whom, in January 1842, 'voluntarily enrolled themselves members of the Birmingham Anti-Corn Law League Association'.[14] In May 1845 the firm manufactured gold and silver buttons in support of the the Anti Corn Law League.[15] The proprietors seem to have sought to iron out differences with their employees. When, in April 1849, a disagreement broke out across the trade over underpayment - known as the 'overcount system' and denounced variously as 'odious' 'cowardly' and 'one of the worst of robberies' – Hammond, Turner & Sons sought to rectify the situation with their own employees.[16] However, wage cuts that autumn led to a strike in the trade; Whateley claimed that the manufacturers were overstating the wages the men earned but was a leading figure in negotiations.[17]

Whateley was not one of the employees who joined the Anti-Corn Law Association, which had been established by local manufacturers and Nonconformist ministers in August 1841.[18] That year he had instead become a member of the congregation of the Chartist Church in Newhall Street which made clear in a resolution that manhood suffrage and not the repeal of the Corn Laws should be the key demand of reformers - and made an offer to explain why this was the case to the ACLA in a discussion, which was not taken up.[19] The opening of the first - and, it transpired, only - Chartist Church in England had come about after discussions

---

[13] *Birmingham Journal,* 4 December 1843, 29 June 1844, 20 June 1846, 5 July 1847, 22 November 1847, 15 October 1849.

[14] Ibid., 29 January 1842.

[15] Ibid., 3 May 1845.

[16] Ibid., 28 April 1849.

[17] Ibid., 22 September 1849.

[18] The president of the ACLA was William Scholefield, who had become mayor after the charter of incorporation came into force in 1838. Its secretary was J.A. Lander, who operated from an office in Colmore Row. Notable supporters included the glass manufacturer Robert Lucas Chance, the button manufacturer W.H. Deykin, the merchant Henry van Wart and the Baptist minister Rev. Thomas Swan.

[19] *Birmingham Journal,* 27 November 1841.

between the Chartist missionary John Collins and Arthur O'Neill in Birmingham and Glasgow in the second half of 1840, and a series of private meetings with like-minded working men which Collins held at his home. Collins was one of the small group of Chartists who rejected the leadership of Feargus O'Connor and his recently-established countrywide organization, the National Charter Association. Of O'Neill's arrival in Birmingham, one Chartist recalled, 'I shall never forget the effect he produced ... wearing his Scottish plaid and looking such a manly, strong and hearty man.'[20] With the backing of Joseph Sturge, a former Swedenborgian chapel was rented. The Chartist Church was intended to be a rival organisation to the local association of the National Charter Association, led by George White, O'Connor's reporter for the *Northern Star*. The NCA group had stronger support, but the congregation at Newhall Street grew to a few hundred, including many young women who learned from O'Neill that they too deserved the vote.[21]

So Whateley found himself listening to O'Neill's sermons each Sunday and attending lectures in Newhall Street on weekday evenings. Members of the church also had access to an extensive library. Tea parties were regularly held – O'Neill urged teetotalism on his congregation and Whateley's life-long abstinence began. Sturge attended the first tea party and, when it was suggested that the working class were unworthy of the vote, memorably replied, 'I will never allow the fears of one man to be the measure of the rights of another.'[22] The reports of these tea parties were in fact intended to demonstrate that working people were fit to vote: they were 'well-dressed and most orderly' and the evenings were 'spent in great good humour and the enjoyment was of the most orderly and rational kind'.[23] There were 350 present for a tea party in September 1841 when Henry Vincent, well-known as an advocate of 'teetotal Chartism', presented Collins 'with a gold watch as a tribute of respect for his services in the Chartist cause'. [24] O'Neill

---

[20] *Kidderminster Times*, 23 December 1876.
[21] From his Chartist years onwards Whateley was also an advocate of extending the vote to women,
[22] *Birmingham Daily Post*, 24 November 1885.
[23] *Birmingham Journal,* 31 July, 2 October 1841.
[24] Ibid.

efforts were not forgotten – he received a Chartist handkerchief and a set of Chartist buttons made by Whateley.

O'Neill said of Whateley that 'he did not know that he ever met with a youth of the industrial class whose acquaintance gave him greater pleasure.'[25] Whateley was an optimistic and committed member of his congregation. He appeared to believe that 'everything he wished for would be accomplished in about seven years.'[26] O'Neill was a printer and so the Chartist Church produced a great number of placards and handbills. Whateley 'rendered him considerable assistance in the matter of printing and circulating pamphlets and other Chartist literature.'[27] When, in summer 1842, strikes across the country against wage cuts were moving towards strikes for the People's Charter, twenty-three year old O'Neill and twenty-year old Whateley threw themselves into the struggle with great energy. 'The crisis is now arrived', a placard signed by O'Neill declared. 'Shall Birmingham, once the polar star of liberty, now slumber? No! Awake! Arise! Stand forward in the nation's moral battle and declare that our country shall now be free![28] Whateley and another member of the O'Neill's congregation were arrested for seeking to put up this placard on walls across the town – though let go after a few hours. If this was meant to serve as a warning to the Chartist Church, it didn't work. Four 'neatly attired' female members of the congregation, 'two of them very young and two middle aged married women', immediately went out with the placards. They were also arrested and, whilst detained, were supplied by supporters with teetotal beverage, fruit and eventually 'a large plate of meat and potatoes'; they agreed to end their activities only 'with much reluctance'.[29]

Whateley was soon feeling as strongly about the wickedness of war as O'Neill, and joined him in supporting his efforts on behalf of the Peace Society. Founded by Quakers in 1816, the Peace Society was to all intents and purposes a pacifist body. The destruction of a British military force by the Afghans in January 1842 greatly alarmed Whateley. 'What shall we do? They will be getting all the

---

[25] *Birmingham Daily Post*, 24 November 1893.
[26] Ibid.
[27] Ibid.
[28] *Birmingham Journal*, 27 August 1842.
[29] Ibid.

young men they can and carrying them off to assist in the vengeance', he told O'Neill. 'What can we do?'[30] What O'Neill and Whateley did was to print many thousands of placards warning young men to keep away from public houses and recruiting offices. When these placards were torn down by the police, the two men went around putting up replacements. Both a Chartist and an anti-war campaigner, O'Neill, speaking at a meeting of striking colliers in Cradley in August 1842, announced that he would not pay income tax to a government which spent money on foreign wars and was arrested. This led to his imprisonment in August 1843 for one year in Stafford Gaol. Temporarily the friendship between Whateley and O'Neill was broken. Though other charismatic men began to exert strong influences on Whateley during these years, it was O'Neill he was always to regard as his chief mentor.

III After Chartism

O'Neill returned quietly to Birmingham in August 1844. Though the Chartist Church had managed to survive during his incarceration, he knew that things could not carry on as before. In June 1846 he was baptized by the Revd. Thomas Swan, the most prominent Baptist minister in the town, and the Chartist Church became a Baptist chapel. By the end of the year O'Neill had baptised over one hundred members of his congregation, including Whateley. The next year these working men and women became part of the Zion Chapel in Newhall Street, led by O'Neill. Whateley, however, soon left, succumbing to the pulling power of George Dawson at the Church of the Saviour. A preacher with many admirers, the Church of the Saviour was erected in Edward Street for Dawson, opening its doors in August 1848 (and often not locking them, leading to periodic thefts of brass railing and hymn books).[31] The Church of the Saviour was non-denominational, its members united in 'oneness of spirit and in a common endeavour to lead the Christian life ... to be a Christian brotherhood, well-instructed and zealous in good works.'[32] Each Sunday, at 11am and 6.30pm, Dawson spelt out this quest from his platform – there was

---

[30] *Birmingham Daily Post*, 24 November 1893.
[31] *Birmingham Journal*, 13 July 1850.
[32] Ibid., 16 August 1851.

no pulpit - and his congregation, accompanied by a paid choir, made use of a volume of hymns and psalms that he had put together. On weekday evenings there were lectures, linking Christian duty with political action.[33] It was later said of Dawson that he 'whipped his congregation into punctuality and order; he cured them of fidgeting; he suppressed needless, noisy coughing; in fact he prided himself on having the best-mannered and "personally conducted" congregation in the town'.[34] The scale of support for Dawson's endeavours was indicated by the numbers he drew in: in March 1851 the average morning congregation stood at 1300 and in August of that year 800 people sat down to tea.[35] Dawson often referred in his sermons and lectures to European struggles for freedom. He had been in Paris in 1848, and also began an admiring correspondence with Lajos Kossuth, ousted in 1849 by an Austrian-Russian army after securing independence for Hungary. All of this Whateley listened to keenly.

Kossuth achieved heroic status in Britain, where he undertook a tour in November 1851.[36] It was said that the crowds that greeted him when, in the middle of the month, he visited Birmingham exceeded those who gathered for the famous reform meeting on Newhall Hill in May 1832. The local Tory paper, estimating that more than 200,000 people assembled to watch his carriage inch its way through the town, reported that 'in many places it was impossible, so great were the numbers, to distinguish the procession from the spectators' and that at Five Ways 'more than half the population of Birmingham appeared to be collected there'.[37] The Hungarian tricolour fluttered from windows and cords decorated with evergreens stretched across streets, Kossuth occasionally rising

[33] For a short time Dawson also edited a weekly newspaper, the *Birmingham Mercury,* described by the *Northern Star,* 9 December 1848, as 'not ... deep enough in colour for our taste ... but we hope to see it supersede the rotten Whig *Journal,* which is a disgrace to Birmingham.'
[34] *Birmingham Daily Gazette,* 29 December 1902.
[35] K. Geary, *The 1851 Census of Religious Worship: Church, Chapel and Meeting Place in Mid Nineteenth Century Warwickshire* (Stratford-upon-Avon, 2014), p. 101; Birmingham Journal, 16 August 1851.
[36] Z. Lada, 'The Invention of a Hero: Lajos Kossuth in England (1851)' in *European History Quarterly* 43:1 2013.
[37] *Aris's Birmingham Gazette,* 17 November 1851; E. Fernie, *Shakespeare for Freedom* (Cambridge, 2017), pp. 28-9.

to bow to the crowds. When Kossuth entered the town hall 'the powerful organ ... was nearly inaudible so deafening were the cheers'.[38] Delighted to be in the same room as such a great man, the audience had no problems whatsoever with listening to him speak for two-and-a-quarter hours. Whateley was thrilled by it all – Dawson had invited him to join the reception committee that greeted Kossuth on his arrival and got him into the Queen's Hotel for the lunch which followed the procession.

Yet Whateley soon defected from the Church of the Saviour – to the People's Baptist Chapel in Great King Street. This was a secession from the Zion Baptist Chapel, which took place soon after O'Neill became pastor. It is now difficult to unravel all these manoeuvrings amongst Birmingham Baptists, but it does seem that Whateley had fallen under the influence of John Skirrow Wright. This man had risen from being an employee to a partner of the military button manufacturers Smith & Kemp. The People's Chapel functioned without a pastor, and Skirrow Wright, who described himself as a teaching elder, often took on the role of preacher. The congregation on a Sunday evening amounted to about 175, all working class people. There were also evening lectures in a school room on the second floor – Skirrow Wright could talk about almost anything, ranging from John Milton to California. 'Wonderful name', the veteran Chartist Thomas Cooper commented of the People's Chapel. 'Can they live up to it?' Whateley certainly tried to: he was known to give money to poorer members of the congregation.

The closure of the Chartist Church did not mean that O'Neill or Whateley ceased to call themselves Chartists. Well into the 1850s a small local Chartist Association met at the Ship Inn in Steelhouse Lane – where, every Sunday at 8pm, it made its contribution to the dramatic events of 1848 by arranging for *Irish Felon* to be read aloud. The leading figures in this group were John Newhouse - who proudly declared that he had been a subscriber to the *Northern Star* since it was first published – James Dumaine – a shoemaker who had been at Newport in 1839 – Allen Dalzeill, John Scrimshire, and John Oxford.[39] Neither Whateley nor O'Neill

---

[38] Ibid.

[39] *Birmingham Journal,* 11 January 1851: Ernest Jones was disappointed by the size of the meeting he addressed: 'Nothing can exceed the apathy

met with these men, though they were present at reform meetings in the town. Thus, at the Public Office in May 1849, O'Neill, sharing a platform with leaders of the local Chartist association, declared that 'there was nothing like going for thorough-going reform at once ... there must be one more mighty agitation and they must see to it that it did the business at once'.[40] A few months later Whateley was at the town hall to hear Dawson, George Muntz and the Chartist stalwart John Mason call for the British government to recognise the independence of the Hungarian people.[41]

And so it continued. If there was a radical meeting in Birmingham in the 1850s, Whateley was in attendance. When, in November 1858, the Birmingham Reform Association was formed, Whateley joined Dawson, Skirrow Wright and George Edmonds on the committee. The BRA sent its propaganda to MPs, lobbied successfully for a town meeting, liaised with reformers in other places and generally sought to back up the work of the recently-returned John Bright in the House of Commons. The Reform League was founded at the beginning of 1865 and Whateley was involved, along with O'Neill and John Oxford, with the Birmingham branch. As the Reform Bill 1867 went through the House of Commons in 1867, he joined in the anger at the ending of compounding by which landlords covered the costs of the rates. The 'trick' went through only for compounding to be reinstated in 1869.[42]

By the 1850s Whateley was part a business partnership with James Rogers, William Broughton and Daniel Grayson. This arrangement may have continued for a period with just Rogers, but eventually Whateley ran his business as a pearl button manufacturer alone.[43] He was able to buy two houses at 354 and 355 Farm Street,

---

and inertness of this large town. I was told it was the largest political audience that had assembled for a long time ... The temper of the meeting was excellent; eighteen members enrolled, a fair proportion out of the number present. Such is democracy in Birmingham.' For the full details of Birmingham Chartism in the 1850s see G. Barnsby, *Birmingham Working People* (Wolverhampton, 1989), pp. 109-124.

[40] *Birmingham Journal*, 19 May 1849.

[41] Ibid., 18 August, 25 August 1849. Mason had arrived in Birmingham as a Chartist lecturer in 1841; soon after this meeting he left for the United States, with a purse of £40 from well-wishers.

[42] *Birmingham Daily Post*, 15 October 1867.

which served as his family residence and his manufactory; in 1861 he was employing twelve men. Whateley sent a case of his pearl buttons to an international exhibition of the craftmanship of working men held in Islington in 1870.[44] Respected by both sides in the trade, he sought to promote cordial relations: in July 1871 he presided over a compromise between men and masters where wages were increased during busy times.[45]

IV A Working Man's Councillor

The Chartist argument that working people had a right to a say in law-making underpinned all that Whateley ever said or did in public life. He carried with him throughout his whole adult life a belief in manhood suffrage and the necessity of working men getting elected to town councils and the House of Commons. He drew attention to the obstacles that stood in the way of working men participating in politics, calling for the abolition of the property qualification that was required to seek election to the town council and for the extension of voting hours until 9pm. When Whateley came forward in Hampton ward in October 1871, it was explicitly as a working man's candidate. Although he was an employer, he stated that 'most of us who are masters in this trade are but a shade higher in the social scale than the men we employ.'[46] Whateley explained that he 'was not for working men being sent into Parliament or municipal bodies with a view to completely overturning the present state of things. He did not believe in their being returned as a sort of Communists and as men who went in for a division of wealth. He simply thought the working classes should be represented as other classes were.'[47] At his meetings Whateley talked of public health being his priority, citing a need for slum clearance, street paving and improved sewers, matters that he declared wealthy councillors living away from the town centre never

---

[43] *Birmingham Journal,* 20 February 1854 lists the dissolution of the partnership of the four men; *Birmingham Daily Post,* 20 November 1893 refers to a longstanding partnership with Turner in Warstone Lane.
[44] Ibid., 21 July 1870; The *Spectator,* 22 October 1870.
[45] *Birmingham Daily Post,* 29 July 1871.
[46] *Birmingham Daily Post,* 15 April 1872
[47] Ibid., 20 October 1871.

gave a thought to. He also declared his support for admission to King Edward's School in New Street for bright working class boys and for shopkeepers in the back streets to be able to put out their goods without police interference – as was the case in the main streets. Whateley had come forward 'to see fair play done to his own class'.[48] When he received the endorsement of another radical stalwart William Radford, the first attempt to return a Chartist to the town council since John Collins a generation earlier was underway.[49]

The other candidate was certainly not a Chartist: Thomas Naish was a decorator who had been re-elected unopposed for twelve years. Naish did not address any public meetings and relied on his attendance record and support for economy. His early departure from a town council meeting that was discussing sewers provided him with an embarrassing episode he did not need. A large section of the congregation of the People's Chapel came out to canvass for Whateley and he was returned with a majority of 126.[50] As a small employer, Whateley wasn't perhaps quite the working man's candidate that he believed himself to be, but – in spite of adjusting his view of trade unions – he was undoubtedly sincere in his desire to represent the interests of working people. [51] It can certainly be said that he paved the way for Lib-Lab trade unionists like J.V. Stevens and Eli Bloor, returned as councillors in the 1880 and 1890s, and Robert Toller, the first independent labour representative in Birmingham, elected in Saltley in 1897.

This proved to be the only electoral contest Whateley faced. Over his twenty-two years on the council, he represented three wards but there were no challenges at election times. Though the uncontested returns of councillors were not unusual in Birmingham, the absence of any attempt to oust him over such a long period points to the strength of support he had. Whateley was certainly conscientious in his attendance at council meetings – for example, in 1883 he was summoned to 89 meetings and attended 84 and in 1886 he was summoned to 88 meetings and attended 81.

---

[48] Ibid.
[49] Ibid., 25 October 1871.
[50] Whateley 1067; Naish 941.
[51] *Birmingham Daily Post,* 4 July 1870. In earlier years Whateley had been a member of the Pearl Button Makers' Society.

The inventor of the 'Pleasant Sunday Afternoon' campaign to promote working class recreation, Whateley sat on the baths and parks committee as well as the lunatic asylums committee and the watch committee, which met fortnightly to receive reports on criminal offences and to consider such matters as police pay, promotions and dismissals. Whateley attended committee and full council meetings with the intention of listening and only contributed when he thought it was absolutely necessary to do so – asking, for example, on one occasion for confirmation of whether large residences in Edgbaston were, unlike other properties, exempt from being charged for the water supply when unoccupied. An analysis of Whateley's voting record during the 1870s illustrates that he was on the Joseph Chamberlain wing of the town council; in 1871-3 he was very much part of the Chamberlain voting network and in 1873-7 only marginally outside the Chamberlain group.[52]

For almost three decades Whateley paid his subscription to the Birmingham Liberal Association. He was never one of Chamberlain's inner circle, and was much closer to his rival Skirrow Wright, the president of the BLA who died in 1880.[53] When the BLA fractured over Irish Home Rule in 1886, he was certainly not torn in his loyalties. Whateley stayed true to Gladstone and his old friend O'Neill and joined the Birmingham Association for the Promotion of Home Rule in Ireland. He was present at several of the well-attended meetings this body organised across the town in 1886. Prominent in this agitation was Lawson Tait, the well-known gynaecological surgeon who was also a councillor.[54] Chamberlain's

---

[52] I am grateful to Les Rosenthal for this information. L. Rosenthal, 'Joseph Chamberlain and the Birmingham Town Council, 1865-1880', *Midland History* 41:1 2016 pp. 71-95 provides a detailed analysis of the voting lists in the minutes of the town council in the years following Chamberlain's election.

[53] S. Roberts, 'John Skirrow Wright: The Benefactor Whose Statue was Destroyed' *Birmingham Historian* 33 2009, pp. 11-15. Whateley played a prominent part in the efforts to raise funds for Skirrow Wright's statue, unveiled in 1883; Richard Tangye had argued for a portrait.

[54] Lawson Tait (1845-1899) was born and educated in Edinburgh and made his name in Birmingham at the hospital for women. Amongst other achievements, he conducted the first removal of an ovary and advanced surgical techniques for the appendix and the gall bladder. He received great encouragement in his work from George Dawson.

supporters did, however, manage to remove Whateley from the presidency of the North Birmingham Liberal Association. One of Whateley's friends described the coup: 'In their estimation the office was too important for Councillor Whateley. They had an enormous number of faults to find with Mr Whateley ... He had no backbone; he is a poor, weak individual, with good intentions enough, but he allows himself to be swayed by those around him ...'[55] Not quite as weak as his opponents claimed, Whateley continued to attend meetings of his local association, on one occasion interrupting a speech made by the Chamberlainite MP for Bordesley Jesse Collings with the cry, '"You joined the Tories"'.[56] Whateley regarded Chamberlain and Collings as nothing less than traitors, describing Joe as 'the man who goes and hobnobs with those who neither toil nor spin and is continually in their society and altogether ignores the people he used to lead.'[57]

Whateley had no doubts that Liberal candidates were 'better able and more willing to serve the interests of working men'.[58] With Chamberlain tightening his grip on Birmingham, Whateley did his best to talk up the chances of the Lib-Lab candidates who came forward in summer 1892. He 'felt sure' and had 'very little doubt' that the trade unionists W.J. Davis and Eli Bloor would be returned, but they were heavily defeated; the Unionist press was delighted to be able to dub Whateley the 'seer of the day'.[59] Despite the jibes, the old Chartist never wavered from his view that 'if the working men only knew and rightly used their power, they would soon truly and directly be represented. They might in the future have real labour representation in Parliament ...'[60]

In the meantime, there were practical steps that could be taken to help working men. The man who in 1872 had raised money amongst the pearl button makers to assist Joseph Arch in his efforts to establish a trade union for farm labourers was in 1884 the president of the Birmingham Postmen's Sunday Rest Association.[61]

---

[55] *Birmingham Daily Post*, 25 April 1887.
[56] Ibid., 1 November 1887.
[57] Ibid., 19 October, 22 October 1888.
[58] Ibid., 30 October 1885.
[59] Ibid., 29 June 1892. Collings, 6380, Davis 2658; Kenrick 4814, Bloor 2089.
[60] Ibid., 23 October 1891.

The aim of this campaign was to end the delivery of letters on Sundays. This had been the practice in London since 1866, but Manchester and Liverpool, like Birmingham, retained Sunday deliveries. A decade earlier the matter had been taken to the town council, but met with determined opposition. When Whateley, T.H. Aston, who served as secretary, and a number of clergymen revived the campaign in 1884, there was again considerable resistance. John Bright countered Whateley's claim that the Sunday post was principally made up of circulars by expressing the view that adult children away from home received letters from their parents on that day. The *Birmingham Daily Post* declared that 'the motive at the bottom of it was sabbatarianism'.[62] With Whateley present, the town council decided to leave things as they were. Whateley believed that the meetings and letters to the newspapers had at least encouraged local people to think carefully about posting material on Saturday evenings and about installing letter boxes rather than expecting postmen to have to knock and wait.[63] Three years later he was again calling for Sunday deliveries, which for postmen were 'wearisome and incessant, involving early rising', to be brought to an end, but thereafter the agitation faded away.[64] The episode clearly indicates that an old Chartist might move towards Liberalism but was not always at ease with what his new allies espoused.

Working men could, of course, seek to improve themselves. Whateley was a member of the Band of Hope Union and the United Kingdom Alliance. These organisations sent out lecturers – there were forty working without payment for the UKA across Birmingham - distributed literature, tested supporters on their understanding of the principles of temperance and lobbied magistrates to reduce the number of licences for public houses. Whateley was a shareholder in, and later a director of, the Birmingham Coffee House Company, established in 1877 'to cover the town with coffee houses'. [65] By the mid-1880s the company had twenty-five branches, employing 160 staff. It was a well-run enterprise – it calculated, for example, that eight customers were

---

[61] Ibid., 15 April 1872. Whateley had pledged £10 but raised £34 19s 1d.
[62] Ibid., 27 October 1884.
[63] Ibid., 21 December 1885, 12 August 1887.
[64] Ibid., 12 December 1887.
[65] Ibid., 28 January 1882; Library of Birmingham, MS 618.

needed for every pound made – and made a good enough profit, particularly in the centre of the town, for the employees to be paid bonuses and the shareholders a dividend of 10%. Whateley was also involved in the New Meeting Provident Society, a less successful operation. Founded in 1836 to provide assistance during periods of illness and with over 700 members, it found itself paying out far more than it expected. The Society chastised itself 'that sufficient care had not been taken in the selection of only healthy and proper persons to be admitted as members and that, after their admission, sufficient care and vigilance had not been taken in watching cases of illness and bringing imposters to punishment'.[66]

Whateley's commitment to temperance and peace had never wavered since his early association with O'Neill. In November 1886 – forty years after the Chartist Church closed – the two men established a Birmingham branch of Workmen's Peace and Arbitration League. O'Neill had spent the intervening decades as an indefatigable lecturer on behalf of the Peace Society, delivering addresses two or three times a week across the midlands.[67] Before Birmingham audiences Whateley condemned the 'alarming' speeches of political leaders, the scale of expenditure on the army and navy and military training in board schools but sincerely believed that they 'were approaching a time when the people would be able to take a better hold of the subject and ... would deal with any government that favoured a blustering war policy in a very different manner to which they had been dealt with in the past.' [68] Whateley was still the man he had been almost half a century earlier when he had gone out on the streets of Birmingham with O'Neill urging working men to avoid recruiting parties.

---

[66] *Birmingham Daily Post,* 27 March 1879.
[67] Roberts, *The Chartist Prisoners,* pp. 155-64.
[68] *Birmingham Daily Post,* 16 November 1886, 17 October 1887, 26 February 1890.

V 'They admired him because he was a Chartist ...'

James Whateley died at his home in Villa Street, Lozells, on 18 November 1893. His wife Mary, a pearl button finisher, had died the previous January. Deeply distraught, his physical health gave out – pneumonia and a fall was followed by a severe stroke, which left him unable to speak or move. His family sang hymns around his bedside; unable to join in, the Christian Chartist managed to beat his hand in time. It fell, of course, to O'Neill to conduct the funeral service at the People's Chapel six days later; admission was by ticket. The procession to Key Hill took place during the lunch hour, and thousands of working people lined the streets for the old Chartist. Recalling his Chartist credentials, one local publication described Whateley as 'a man with backbone in him ... a sturdy radical, one of the Old Guards, who never bowed the knee to Joseph ...'[69] At the next meeting of the city council the mayor remembered his independence of mind: '... during his long period of service Mr Whateley always formed a clear and honest opinion upon every question ... and ... always acted with unswerving loyalty towards his friends. When he had the misfortune to differ from them, it was never in the spirit of factious opposition but because he honestly believed the cause he advocated was the best.'[70] A plan that his eldest son should take his place on the city council came to nothing, and he was replaced by a Tory, 'the flabby chairman of the Chamber of Commerce' J.W. Tonks.[71] Whateley would have been horrified. A few months later his family put up for sale his entire stock of 3,500 pearl buttons.

James and Mary Whateley were the parents of nine sons and two daughters; three of these children died in infancy. At the time of their deaths they had an astonishing thirty-nine grandchildren and one great grandchild. Their eldest child was Joseph, born in

---

[69] The *Owl*, 1 December 1893.
[70] *Birmingham Daily Post*, 6 December 1893; the *Owl*, 27 November 1893; the *Dart*, 1 December 1893, described Tonks as 'the chosen candidate of the *Post*, the *Mail* and Joseph for the seat left vacant by the death of the old radical, Whateley ... (He) will ... vote as the *Post*, the *Mail* and Joseph tell him. The old gospel changeth not: "Vote as you are told"'
[71] Ibid. The Liberals organised a meeting to select a candidate 'but only three members attended and nothing was done.'

1847; their youngest surviving child was Oliver, born in 1862. The second son James (1850-1904) became a dentist, and adopted the name of his German wife Hermine Clemencon: their daughter Haidee became a singer and comedian. Their third and fourth sons George (b. 1852) and Edgar (b. 1855) and second daughter Alice (b. 1854) entered the pearl button trade (which was in decline) and their fifth and sixth sons Alfred and Albert became respectively a case maker and a gem seller. Only one child celebrated his father's political affiliations – their eighth son John, born in 1860, the year that Italy secured unification, was given the second name of Garibaldi.

Oliver Whateley – known as Olly – was a lithographer, pianist and singer and footballer. He designed the illuminated addresses presented to leading Birmingham Liberals, including Richard and George Tangye in December 1885, and played for Aston Villa from 1881 until 1887.[72] He was a prolific goal scorer, a specialist in 'quick, low shots' which earned him great popularity amongst Villa supporters and the nickname 'Daisycutter'.[73] Twice capped for England, he scored on his debut. Up to 9,000 spectators would gather on a Saturday afternoon at Perry Barr to watch the Villa. Amongst them was the inside left's father, Councillor James Whateley, the old Chartist.[74]

---

[72] Ibid., 31 December 1885, 1 October 1886.

[73] *Nottingham Evening Post,* 22 November 1890. As well as being able to deliver 'a warm shot' and 'a hot one', Whateley was also noted for his 'pretty dribbling' and 'brilliant tackling' (*Birmingham Daily Post,* 13 March, 16 October, 27 October 1882, 19 March 1883).

[74] *Birmingham Daily Post,* 20 June 1887, for Whateley's attendance with his son at the annual dinner of the Birmingham and District Football Association. After he left Aston Villa Oliver Whateley re-located to London and during the First World War served with the YMCA in France. His later years were blighted by ill-health and poverty and, in 1923, Aston Villa sought donations for a fund to help him. He died in Birmingham in October 1926 and was buried in Witton cemetery.

III. The Chartist Minister: Charles Clarke (1820-1892)

Twenty years after its demolition the Unitarian Old Meeting House in New Street, Birmingham, was remembered as being in 'a dirty, dingy, unwholesome locality; yet, on Sundays, carriages would roll into the dull, narrow street and Birmingham's most noted and wealthy citizens would step out to attend meeting house services'.[1] What drew so many of the most prominent families of the town – amongst them the Scholefields, the Martineaus and the Nettlefolds - to this Unitarian chapel was the preaching of its minister, Charles Clarke. In a town famous for its preachers, Clarke was one of the most gifted. Contemporary reports often referred to his rhetorical talents - 'his usual clear and emphatic style' and so on – and his eloquence can still be detected in the published versions of his sermons.[2] 'Unitarians believe that under all circumstances one and one are two', he would remark of the need for clarity, 'and two and one are three'.[3] From the pulpit he linked Christian belief with high standards of personal behaviour and with political freedom and civic duty. In one sermon he observed that many his congregation were 'held in honour on account of their public spirit, their labours for the public good, their anxiety to do what they could for the prudent, wise and economical government and progress of Birmingham and the maintenance of its charitable and educational institutions'.[4] During the first two decades of Clarke's tenure no fewer than six mayors emerged from his congregation.[5] The messages of his sermons were reinforced by

---

[1] *Birmingham Daily Gazette*, 29 December 1902.

[2] *Birmingham Journal*, 8 November 1856; C. Clarke, *Street Preaching* (1856); Old Meeting House, Birmingham *A Sermon Preached before the Teachers and Scholars* (1864); *Religion and Legislation* (1876); *Salvation* (1881). Copies of these published sermons can be found in the Library of Birmingham.

[3] *Birmingham Daily Gazette*, 29 December 1902.

[4] *Birmingham Daily Post*, 15 March 1882.

[5] James Baldwin was elected mayor in 1853. A paper manufacturer, he was a great admirer of William Cobbett and a member of the Birmingham Political Union, the Association for the Promotion of the Repeal of the Taxes on Knowledge and the Reform League. He was well known for breeding pigs. John Palmer was elected mayor in 1854. He was a wine

regular lectures either at the Old Meeting House or the Birmingham and Midland Institute. When this man arrived in Birmingham in May 1852, at the age of thirty-two, he was far from a stranger to public speaking; he had shaped his beliefs and honed his oratorical skills as a Chartist in south-west England.

I 'Our Sacred Principles': Bath 1833-45

Clarke was a free-thinking Chartist. Though deeply loyal to 'our sacred principles', he raised the idea of a phased extension of the franchise and later made clear his unease about the strategy of class confrontation advocated by Feargus O'Connor.[6] It was in Bath, at the age of seventeen or eighteen, that he first began attending Chartist meetings. Born in Milborne Port in south Somerset, he had been sent the forty miles to Bath at the age of thirteen by his father, a glove manufacturer, to be apprenticed in a family friend's ironmongery business. Studious and religious, Clarke read widely in theology, history and poetry and attended services in a number of chapels before settling on the Unitarians. For the rest of his life the principles of rational reflection and social justice that he found in Unitarianism shaped all he thought and said.

In John Arthur Roebuck, Clarke saw the ideal type of political leader. One of the MPs for Bath from 1832-7 (and again from 1841-9), Roebuck was a radical journalist who argued for a significant extension of the franchise and a national system of compulsory elementary education. He set out these objectives in speeches in his constituency and also in his *Pamphlets for the People* (1835-6). Clarke was present at the public meetings, and also read the pamphlet series. These issues remained at the core of

---

merchant and one of the men who arranged for John Bright to stand for Birmingham in 1858. Henry Holland was elected mayor in 1868. He was a manufacturer of parts for umbrellas. Thomas Prime was elected mayor in 1869. He ran an electro-plating business: amongst the items he produced was a medallion and a bust in memory of, respectively, Thomas Attwood and Joseph Sturge. John Sadler was elected mayor in 1871. He was a major shareholder in a gas company. Ambrose Biggs was elected mayor in 1872. He was a tobacco merchant. Arthur Ryland, a solicitor who was elected mayor in 1860, had worshipped at the Old Meeting House but joined George Dawson's Church of the Saviour in 1848.

6 *Northern Star,* 19 February 1842.

Clarke's beliefs for the rest of his life: the man who gave lectures to the Bath Chartists on the power of knowledge became in Birmingham one of the most persevering advocates of education for the people. Coming from the background he did, Clarke saw possibilities in a cross-class reform alliance and dangers in the confrontational strategy advocated by O'Connor.

Doubtless Clarke's own talents as a wordsmith contributed to his confidence in persuasion and rational argument. In a series of eloquent front-page articles for the *Charter* – a journal set up by the London Chartists in 1839-40 – he informed 'my brother Chartists' that 'no bloody insurrection is necessary ... a vigorous dissemination of Chartist principles is all that is necessary.'[7] This was to be achieved by the establishment of a Chartist daily newspaper, the distribution of tracts and lecture tours. Faced by 'an irresistible combination of the middle and working classes', manhood suffrage would be implemented, even if it was in phases (an idea he soon quietly abandoned).[8]

This 'rather tall, slim, dark-haired young fellow' began to travel throughout the west of England as a Chartist missionary.[9] He became a full time working class politician, abandoning his apprenticeship and living off the movement as a journalist and a lecturer. In chapels and in the open air, he led prayers, read aloud from the Bible and advocated the need for self-improvement in knowledge and personal behaviour as the means of securing a place for working men in the constitution. For thirty years from his pulpit in Birmingham, he set out the same message – although his athleticism on one occasion in Wiltshire, when he climbed a pole in front of the platform at a protectionist meeting in order to make a speech, was not to be called on in later years.

In public Clarke remained loyal to O'Connor. He joined the National Charter Association and, when the Chartist leader arrived in Bath in December 1841 to address a meeting, it was Clarke who moved the vote of thanks.[10] However, relations between the two

---

[7] Quoted in Roberts, *Radical Politicians and Poets*, pp. 78-9. I first told Clarke's story, with only a brief consideration of his Birmingham years, in ibid., pp. 77-88.
[8] Ibid., p. 79.
[9] Ibid., p. 77.
[10] *Northern Star*, 24 December 1841.

men were no so cordial in private. Clarke raised the question of educating the people and O'Connor 'turned on him, fiercely exclaiming "Damn their education" and swung round on his heel ...'[11] It was the breach that perhaps both men wanted. By this point Clarke was openly aligning himself with the Chartist lecturer and editor Henry Vincent. The *National Vindicator,* a weekly publication that Vincent produced from Bath, advocated education, teetotalism and class collaboration. Another prominent Bath Chartist Robert Kemp Philp, a fellow Unitarian and close in age to Clarke, was moving in the same direction.[12] Clarke made clear that he still regarded himself as a Chartist but declared that 'we should not be jealous of the middle classes, we should receive the overtures they had made to us as being a great advance for the Charter.'[13] It was a stance that O'Connor's *Star* could not stomach and readers were advised that Clarke 'is among the tail of the once professedly unchanging, firm-until-death, energetic, flaming, Chartist Henry Vincent'.[14]

Highly successful in his anti-slavery agitation, the Quaker Joseph Sturge had, in spring 1842, launched an attempt to build a cross-class alliance through his Complete Suffrage Union. Clarke – who knew nothing of the deeply-embedded class consciousness of the manufacturing areas of the north - was intimately involved, attending early meetings of the provisional council. His main work for the new cause was as a paid lecturer in the west of England.[15] The support of working class leaders like Clarke and Philp was essential to the success of the enterprise. A delegate to both CSU conferences in Birmingham in April and December 1842, Clarke was deployed to reassure both sides. To the middle class delegates he explained that violent working class protest emanated from poverty: '... let them imagine themselves without food, willing to work and having none to do, with a wife and children starving for want ... then perhaps they might be able to realise the feelings which

---

[11] Roberts, *Radical Politicians and Poets,* p. 81.
[12] M. Chase, 'An Overpowering "Itch for Writing": R.K. Philp, John Denman and the Culture of Self-Improvement', *English Historical Review,* 133, 2018.
[13] Roberts, *Radical Politicians and Poets,* p. 81.
[14] *Northern Star,* 24 December 1842.
[15] *Western Times,* 1 October 1842.

prompted violence.'[16] To the Chartist delegates he offered understanding of their predicament: '... many Chartists were in a very peculiar situation; they had advocated the Charter for many years and were pledged to it ...'[17] There seems little doubt that Clarke would have accepted the substitution of Sturge's Bill of Rights for the People's Charter; but, in a rare alliance, O'Connor and William Lovett obliterated this new move.

II 'To Preach Politics alike in the Pulpit and on the Platform': Canterbury and Glasgow, 1847-1852

With the collapse of Sturge's plans, Clarke continued to work as a professional lecturer. As before, he operated in the west of England. Widely read, he was able to talk about a range of historical and literary subjects, and he was also employed by the Anti-Corn Law League. When he was not lecturing, he was preaching. Another Unitarian preacher and CSU lecturer, with whom Clarke formed a strong friendship, was Henry Solly. It was Solly who recommended him as minister to the Unitarian congregation in Shepton Mallet, near Bath. This was a temporary position – with a very healthy salary of £125 - whilst Solly completed his duties elsewhere. Clarke was 'much liked' and Solly was able to recommend him as the permanent minister for Canterbury.[18] Whether he was in the pulpit or on the platform, Clarke's addresses demonstrated considerable reading and thought and were delivered with great expressiveness. He had always known that public speaking was the role he was best-suited for, but now it was no longer a precarious way of leading his life. He soon made his mark in Canterbury. At the Philosophical Institute, in a 'pleasing, yet forcible, manner', he endorsed phrenology, arguing that it was of great use to parents and teachers.[19] He went on to consider personal behaviour, describing crime as 'a moral disease ... he trusted ere long that our prisons, instead of being nurseries of vice, would be converted into moral hospitals.'[20] In conclusion Clarke urged his

---

[16] Roberts, *Radical Politicians and Poets*, p. 82.

[17] Ibid., p. 83.

[18] H. Solly, *These Eighty Years* (1893), I, p. 430.

[19] *Canterbury Journal*, 1 February 1845.

[20] Ibid.

audience to understand why those whose behaviour they disapproved of were as they were – they should, he sympathetically observed, adopt 'a lenient bearing towards the delinquencies of others, especially the poor ... we ought ... to take into consideration the influence by which many an unfortunate fellow is surrounded.'[21]

When, in 1847, Solly declined an offer to become Unitarian minister in Glasgow – 'my wife and myself feared the climate' – he again suggested Clarke for the vacancy.[22] Clarke was still unmarried, but in Glasgow this situation changed. In June 1847 he married Mary Dunn; born in Somerset and the daughter of a tailor, she was a member of his congregation. Their first child, Florence, was born three years later.

The congregation of the Union Street Chapel was able to purchase for 1s 2d a volume entitled *Hymns and Anthems* which Clarke compiled. He followed his Sunday morning sermons with lectures on history, literature and other subjects he had mastered, including astronomy and phonetics. These lectures were infused with his radical beliefs. At one lecture he declared that working people 'were entirely at the mercy of the capitalist' and that 'it was absurd that 30,000 people should possess the lands of this country and allow immense tracts to be waste whilst the populations of rural districts were being driven into the towns to make room for hares, partridges and other animals for the amusement of our aristocracy'.[23] At another lecture he re-interpreted the definition of divine right as not 'the old idea by which kings lorded it over their subjects but ... the election by the people of the best and wisest men to affairs of political trust'.[24] His congregation were left in no doubt that their minister was still a Chartist.

In fact Clarke was prepared to go further than simply urging the Unitarians of Glasgow to embrace the principles of the People's Charter. In March 1851, at a meeting at the East Regent Street Chapel, he was elected as a delegate to a Chartist convention in London. Amidst what he described as the 'howlings' of Clarke's supporters, a veteran Glasgow Chartist, the shoemaker Daniel Paul, was rejected for the role. [25] Unlike Clarke, he had been unable to

---

[21] Ibid.
[22] H. Solly, *These Eighty Years,* p. 431.
[23] *Glasgow Sentinel,* 8 February 1851.
[24] Ibid., 15 February 1851.

disassociate himself from O'Connor and was also accused of paying low wages. Calling a meeting of his own, he declared that he paid his workmen fairly and that though 'no partisan or unreflecting friend of Mr O'Connor's ... he believed he was a true patriot and ... did not like to hear the name of such a man blasphemed.'[26] Paul turned up in London anyway and a committee of the convention declared him elected to represent Glasgow.[27] Unwilling to be involved in a wrangle, Clarke had not bothered to travel. So Clarke was not to re-enter the world of Chartist politics, but he continued to promote democratic ideas. 'As often as I read the *Penny Cyclopedia*', he wrote after the presentation that marked his departure for Birmingham in May 1852, 'I shall remember the opportunities I enjoyed in Glasgow of speaking in support of principles for which it is a reward in itself to be permitted to speak.'[28]

III 'A Protest in this Town on Behalf of Liberty of Conscience': Birmingham 1852-1882

There had been a Unitarian congregation in Birmingham since the late seventeenth century. Their radical religious and political beliefs made their chapels targets for Church and King mobs: the Unitarian chapel in Birmingham was partially destroyed during riots in 1715 and completely destroyed during the Priestley riots of July 1791.[29] The Old Meeting House in New Street, Birmingham, was built – at a cost of £4,500 – as a replacement and opened in October 1795. The brick-built chapel, capable of seating 1,100

---

[25] Ibid., 5 April 1851. Daniel Paul often chaired Chartist meetings in Glasgow in 1848 and the years following; *Northern Star*, 13 July 1850, for a letter from him praising O'Connor for, amongst other things, 'your conduct at the Kennington Common meeting for not leading the people on to be murdered.'

[26] *Glasgow Sentinel*, 5 April 1851. The *Penny Cyclopedia* was published by the Society for the Diffusion of Useful Knowledge.

[27] *Northern Star*, 5 April 1851.

[28] *Glasgow Sentinel*, 19 June 1852.

[29] K.R. Johnston, *Usual Suspects: Pitt's Reign of Alarm & the Lost Generation of the 1790s* (Oxford, 2013), pp. 47-63 is the most recent account of these events, in which almost thirty properties, including the house of the chemist and radical Joseph Priestley, and four chapels were destroyed over five days.

people, was 'at the time described as ... very handsome ... but we would not now call it handsome', observed a member of the congregation shortly before its demolition.[30] The congregation certainly included those with means: in summer 1859 £535 was raised for repairs to the chapel and another £203 18s 6d for the General Hospital. With the departure of Hugh Hutton for Suffolk, Clarke became the sixth minister at the new chapel. Hutton, who had been in place for twenty-nine years, had openly preached radicalism and had composed the hymn 'The Gathering of the Unions' that was sung at the great Newhall Hill reform meeting in May 1832. He was a hard act to follow, but the invitation had been issued to Clarke as a result of his reputation in Unitarian circles as a conscientious and inspiring preacher.

The new minister began to make changes: a new hymn book, compiled by the Unitarian scholar James Martineau, was adopted (1852); an organ was installed to accompany the choir instead of a violin and clarinet (1854); a chapel journal was launched (1855); and a new pulpit and improved heating was put in (1857).[31] What Clarke said in his sermons and lectures was heard across the town. When the Rev. J.C. Miller, the rector of St. Martin's, declared, in a lecture in April 1854, that working men were turning their backs on Unitarianism, the Old Meeting was 'densely crowded' for a series of lectures in which Clarke courteously replied to his 'misrepresentations ... and ... fallacious reasonings'.[32] Three thousand copies of these lectures were printed for distribution across the town. That year Clarke's lecture at the Old Meeting in support of the Crimean War was also published. He argued that Britain was fighting a just war against Russian tyranny:

'I think we are called by God to oppose Russia ... Russian despotism, from its very nature, will absorb all it can ... As it will observe no conditions, Providence imposes on free states the duty of crushing or chaining it ... Is our rank to be upheld? Is the balance of power in Europe

---

[30] C. H. Beale, *Memorials of the Old Meeting House and Burial Ground, Birmingham* (Birmingham, 1882), p. 39.

[31] An incomplete run of the *Old Meeting House Journal,* issued from 1855 until 1857, can be found in the Library of Birmingham.

[32] *Aris's Birmingham Gazette,* 10 April 1854; *Birmingham Journal,* 20 May 1854. Samuel Bache, minister of the New Meeting House, was also involved in rebutting Miller.

to be preserved? These are the questions which we are to answer. Personally, I know that Great Britain ought not to permit her relative weight and influence to be altered by means of the invasion of one Empire by another. They say that this is selfish; perhaps it is. I contend, nevertheless, that religion sanctions this course of self-defence ...'[33]

Clarke was far from alone amongst Chartists in believing that Russian absolutism had to be confronted. His endorsement of the war was followed by a collection amongst his congregation for the families of British soldiers [34]

Clarke subscribed throughout his life to the Unitarian and Chartist beliefs that working people needed knowledge to claim their democratic rights and to lead useful and contented lives. Education was, he declared, 'the great necessity of our times ...'[35] Three years after he became minister a school room was built at the rear of the chapel at cost of £727. This was to be very well used - by the Sunday School, by classes for reading, writing and arithmetic which met on weekday evenings and by Clarke for his regular lectures. By early 1865 there were 355 boys and 169 girls in the Sunday School. They were taught separately and classes were small as Clarke managed to recruit a good supply of teachers from his congregation. Each Christmas these children attended a tea, at which there were recitations and songs, each one of them, on leaving, being supplied with an apple and an orange. It was Clarke's hope that these young people would eventually attend classes at the Birmingham and Midland Institute – those who did so, in 1868-9, were able to listen to a history of England from the lips of their minister. Clarke also organised a singing class in the school room, which soon recruited 150 male singers, all paying 1d a week to participate.

At the Old Meeting House Clarke's lectures ranged across the history of Protestantism, theology, philosophy and poetry. Admission to these lectures was free, but there was a charge of one penny to attend readings – at which Clarke himself often did most of the reading. During winter 1858-9, for example, he read selections from Milton (a favourite lecture topic), Shakespeare and

---

[33] Roberts, *Radical Politicians and Poets*, p. 84.
[34] *Aris's Birmingham Gazette*, 24 April 1854.
[35] Ibid., 8 November 1856.

Carlyle - and, at the last meeting before Christmas, the entirety of Dickens' *A Christmas Carol*. He was a regular lecturer at the Polytechnic Institute and, after it closed in 1853, at the Birmingham and Midland Institute, usually choosing authors and philosophers as his subjects.[36] Like George Dawson - whose place he filled at the Church of the Saviour during a period of illness in autumn 1868 - Clarke adored Shakespeare:

'He devoted himself to the illustration of human life ... He was true to nature and showed how guilt invariably brought its punishment. To be consistent, those who object, should object also to the Bible ... This great Shakespeare -deeply earnest, rationally devout, setting down the many-coloured story of man's life ... telling out the things he knew - made them see that in the universe there was nothing common, nothing which might not be used in fulfilment of a Divine purpose for the support and encouragement of good.'[37]

After 1866 Clarke was introduced at his lectures as a Fellow of the Linnean Society. It was the only academic honour this working class devotee of knowledge ever received.

Clarke sought to influence public policy from behind his lectern. His duties as a minister allowed him only a little time to attend meetings outside his chapel. He did, however, play a leading role in the local campaign against the Nuisances Removal and Diseases Prevention Bill in spring 1855. Introduced as a consequence of the cholera epidemic of 1853-4, the Bill sought to compel town councils to employ sanitary inspectors and enter properties that contained nuisances. Joining with Joseph Allday, who led a group known as the economists on the town council, Clarke offered his 'most determined opposition.'[38] For Clarke the objection was about centralisation - as it had been when, as a

---

[36] R.E. Waterhouse, *The Birmingham and Midland Institute* (Birmingham, 1954); *Birmingham Journal*, 23 April 1854; *Aris's Birmingham Gazette*, 24 April 1854. The Polytechnic Institution opened in Steelhouse Lane in 1843. It recruited over 800 members and offered classes for different levels of ability, a reading room and a library, but was superseded by the Birmingham and Midland Institute, founded by Act of Parliament in 1854.

[37] *Birmingham Daily Post*, 26 October 1876.

[38] *Aris's Birmingham Gazette*, 30 April 1855.

Chartist journalist, he protested against the Rural Police Act of 1839. He summed up his deeply-felt opposition with the declaration that the Bill 'was opposed to the constitution and to our habits of self-government ... the General Board (of Health) in London would have entire power and control over all local affairs ... the town council would be entirely set aside. The General Board would have the power to invade the town ...'[39] Speeches were made, a petition sent to the town's MPs George Muntz and William Scholefield - and the Bill was passed into law.

Like so many Chartists, Clarke saw a clear line of continuity between 'our sacred principles' and Gladstonian Liberalism. He joined the Birmingham Liberal Association when it was established in 1865, playing an active part in the campaigning of the Edgbaston ward committee and becoming one of the '600' (the general committee of the BLA). The Chartists had often called for improved organisation, and Clarke was greatly impressed by efficient and effective way the BLA operated; 'it was', he informed one audience, 'only by acting on the instructions the committee had given that they had a right to look for success'.[40] He was sure they lived in times of progress. 'He looked upon it as a great honour to be able to serve the Liberals', he observed. 'They had put into their hands by means of extending the suffrage a powerful instrument by which the most important changes might be brought about.'[41] The Birmingham Liberal politician with whom Clarke had the closest relationship was George Dixon, whom he had got to know through the Edgbaston and Birmingham Debating Society. Dixon shared his concern for improved education. With the death of William Scholefield, there was a by-election in July 1868 and Dixon came forward. Like George Dawson, Clarke addressed meetings in support of Dixon. 'Combining a personal character of the highest excellence with the most advanced principles', he declared, 'Mr Dixon had every claim for their confidence. He hoped Mr Dixon would have a triumphant election.'[42] Dixon did indeed have a triumphant election, securing 1600 more votes than the Tory banker Sampson Lloyd.[43] In the general election which followed

---

[39] Ibid.
[40] *Birmingham Daily Gazette*, 16 November 1868.
[41] *Birmingham Daily Post*, 16 November 1868.
[42] Ibid.

the next year Dixon headed the Birmingham poll and Gladstone became Prime Minister. To Clarke's great satisfaction, the first piece of legislation brought forward by Gladstone was the disestablishment of the Irish Church. Thereafter Clarke was to regularly speak in support of Liberal candidates in municipal elections. In November 1873 he appeared on behalf of his friend James Deykin to denounce the Tories as 'boobies'; Deykin, denying Tory allegations that he had embraced Unitarianism, secured a handsome victory.[44]

During these years Birmingham came to the fore as the town most earnestly striving to improve the provision of schooling for working class children. This was largely due to George Dixon, who called the meetings that led to establishment of the Birmingham Education Society in 1867 and the National Educational League in 1869. Clarke served on the committees of both these organisations – along with Dawson, Chamberlain and the Congregationalist minister R.W. Dale. He was already a diligent supporter of the Protestant Dissenting Charity School in Graham Street, which providing free schooling for 40-50 poor girls destined for domestic service.[45] The BES, with a paid secretary and an office in New Street, collected statistics which greatly alarmed Clarke: 48% of school age children were neither at school or work.[46] The BES used some of the funds it raised from its subscriptions and donations – it raised £1,012 14s 4d at the time of its launch - to pay the fees of poor children and enlarge existing schools, but it was clear to Dixon and Clarke that a national campaign to transform elementary education was needed.[47] It has been suggested that the six objectives of the NEL were inspired by the People's Charter.[48] Whether this was the case or not, Clarke certainly believed utterly in compulsory, free, secular schooling. Across the town – and also as an occasional

---

[43] J. Dixon, *Out of Birmingham: George Dixon (1820-98)* (2013), pp. 69-72.

[44] S. Roberts, *Joseph Gillott and Four Other Birmingham Manufacturers 1784-1892* (Birmingham, 2016), pp. 55-6.

[45] *Birmingham Journal*, 30 January 1867.

[46] J. Dixon, *Out of Birmingham: George Dixon*, p. 83.

[47] *Birmingham Journal*, 22 June 1867.

[48] J. Dixon, *Out of Birmingham: George Dixon*, p. 90.

missionary - Clarke promoted the principles of the NEL at public meetings.[49]

The intellectual elite of Birmingham rallied around the educational and charitable institutions of the town. Like Dawson, Sam Timmins and J.T. Bunce, Clarke was a shareholder – known as a proprietor – in the Birmingham Library in Union Street. Founded in 1779, this institution had strong connections with Joseph Priestley. Only shareholders who paid an annual subscription of 30s had access, but in 1860 membership was extended with the creation of guinea subscribers. In 1873 Clarke was elected to the management committee and then, in 1875, as president of the Birmingham Library, which by this time had 1300 members and about 40,000 volumes.[50] The Birmingham Library served the needs of the middle class, and Clarke was therefore concerned that he did all he could to support the Central Lending and Reference Library, opened in 1865-6. For many years he attended meetings of the management committee set up by the town council. This committee – which also included men such as Timmins and Bunce – supervised the purchase of books, of which at the end of the first decade there were 44,000 for reference and 17,500 for loan.[51] Clarke was conscientious in his attendance: he was called to 22 meetings in 1876-77 and attended 17.[52] He continued in this role until November 1886. The Queen's Hospital in Bath Row, a building of four storeys, opened in 1840. In January 1869, at a meeting in the town hall chaired by Dawson, a plan was adopted to build an extension with subscriptions raised by working men. Clarke was chairman of the committee of management at this point and the new building was opened in November 1873. [53]

IV Final Years

---

[49] *Birmingham Daily Post,* 2 March 1870, 18 October 1871, 10 April 1872.

[50] Ibid., 13 October 1870, 24 February, 9 December 1875; J.A. Langford, *Birmingham: A Handbook* (1879), pp. 69-70.

[51] Ibid., pp. 62-6.

[52] *Birmingham Daily Post,* 11 November 1873, 3 October 1877.

[53] Ibid., pp. 131-3; *Birmingham Daily Mail,* 2 September 1871; *Birmingham Daily Post,* 30 January, 20 December 1871.

Clarke and his congregation 'had long thought the chapel too near to the railway to be safe.'[54] The London and North-Western Railway had made an attempt to purchase the Old Meeting in 1875 – but the congregation had successfully resisted this. When the LNWR came back four years later, it was reluctantly decided that opposition to the proposed Act of Parliament to extend New Street railway station would be 'useless and leave them with heavy expenses to pay.'[55] So in December 1881 the Old Meeting was sold for £30,000. Clarke preached for the final time in March 1882, and soon after the chapel was demolished.[56] The bodies in the burial ground - which had been closed since 1873 – were exhumed and re-interred in Witton cemetery. To mark his twenty years as minister in May 1872 Clarke had been presented with a clock and £300; now, in settlement of a claim for disturbance, the LNWR paid him £2,000. The congregation set aside £20,000 to build a new chapel in Bristol Road, but Clarke, now sixty-two years old, decided to retire.

For a few more years Clarke remained active on the religious and political scene in Birmingham. He accepted invitations to preach, and offered his services as secretary of organisations associated with Unitarianism. He continued to attend Liberal meetings, though, in 1886, like his fellow Chartist Thomas Cooper, he found himself unable to support Irish Home Rule and broke with Gladstone, whom he had so long admired. Deciding not to withdraw from politics, Clarke joined the Birmingham Liberal Unionist Association. His eldest son, Hubert (1853-1917), who became a Unitarian minister at different locations in the north of England before a final move to Surrey, remained a Liberal. Educated at King Edward's School in Birmingham and Manchester New College, he was known as 'a man of wide classical and literary knowledge'.[57] He died unmarried in January 1917, aged 63. Clarke's fourth son Percy (1861-1920), the father of five children, became the long-serving editor of the *Bristol Mercury,* a Liberal

---

[54] C.H. Beale, *Memorials of the Old Meeting House,* p. 42.
[55] Ibid.
[56] Reports of the annual meetings of the congregation of the Old Meeting House for 1868, 1875, 1878-9 and 1881-2 can be found in the Library of Birmingham.
[57] *Surrey Advertiser,* 29 January 1917.

morning newspaper, which was widely read in south-west England and south Wales.[58]

Just as securing the franchise for men had been of the utmost importance to Clarke, so securing the franchise for women was to his wife. Mary Clarke was a member of the Birmingham branch of the National Society for Women's Suffrage. The leading local figures in this campaign were Eliza Sturge, the niece of Joseph Sturge, and Hannah Crosskey, wife of Henry Crosskey, from 1869 minister of the Unitarian Church of the Messiah in Broad Street. These women distributed pamphlets and collected signatures for petitions – in March 1886 George Dixon presented a petition signed by 4,707 Birmingham female householders.[59] Clarke's daughters also become involved in local politics, canvassing on behalf of Liberal candidates in School Board elections.

Ill-health ensured that Clarke was rarely seen in his final years. He turned to his favoured homeopathic medicines, but died of bronchitis on 15 November 1892. He was interred in Witton cemetery, leaving an estate worth £3,274 14s 9d.[60] Clarke had done his best for the causes he had advocated since his Chartist days. Spurning overtures that he stand for Parliament, he found his radical niche as a progressive minister. Setting aside men such as William Hill or Arthur O'Neill, who already presided over chapels during the Chartist period, Clarke appears to have been the only former Chartist who went on to become a minister. Speaking from the pulpit or the platform suited him. He was, he said late in his life, 'ready if wanted: he could write, he could teach; he could stand by the great Liberal cause in religion, in politics and science, and express, in ways which were open, one man's earnest devotion to it ...'[61]

---

[58] Obit: *Western Daily Press,* 20 February 1920. Of Clarke's other children, Florence (1851-1916) did not marry and worked as a governess and French teacher; Alfred (b. 1856) married, fathered one son and worked as an optician in Southampton; Robert (b. 1859) did not marry and worked as a solicitor in Birmingham; and Mary (1865-1943) did not marry and became a head teacher in Birmingham.

[59] *Birmingham Daily Post,* 20 May 1886.

[60] Obits: ibid., 17 November 1892; *Christian Life and Unitarian World,* 19 November 1892; *Inquirer,* 26 November 1892. Mary Clarke pre-deceased her husband; his estate was divided between his son Hubert and his two unmarried daughters

61 *Birmingham Daily Post*, 15 March 1882.

IV. The Survival of Chartism

In my sixth form days I read an observation - I cannot now remember by whom but I am fairly sure it was by a noted historian – that, a generation after the death of Feargus O'Connor in 1855, Chartism was almost forgotten. This claim would not be made now. Chartism undoubtedly left a potent legacy in many communities across Britain. The processions and meetings and the *Northern Star* and Feargus O'Connor were to be long recalled. In Sunderland the wife of the Chartist bookseller James Williams was able to draw on 'a wonderful store of recollections'; and in Kirriemuir the stories of James Donald 'about the local leaders were very entertaining and amusing'.[1] Leading figures in the movement began to tell their own stories in newspapers and books, and R.G. Gammage's *History of the Chartist Movement* was re-published in an extensively-revised edition in 1894. Chartist banners were retrieved and displayed in reform demonstrations, particularly in 1884-5; letters or donations to radical causes were attributed in provincial newspapers to 'An Old Chartist'.

The men who had addressed the meetings and arranged for the placards to be posted and the signatures to be collected often remained prominent figures in their communities. They became local spokesmen, continuing to draw their legitimacy from public meetings, or elected councillors. In Barnsley Frank Mirfield addressed meetings in support of lower meat prices and a cleaner water supply. Many – Henry Ainsworth in Clithero and William Bell in Heywood are examples - became active in the co-operative movement. Some became newspaper editors. James Williams – who was also elected to the town council – became the proprietor of the *Sunderland Times.* Abel Hinchcliffe and Bernard Dromgoole became, respectively, the editors of the *Grimsby Observer* and the *St. Helens' Advertiser.* Described as 'a grand old man of the Chartists', Hinchcliffe 'converted a Tory organ into a democratic organ of the most advanced type'.[2] These men, in early adulthood during the 1840s, acquired as Chartists the self-confidence and the

---

[1] *Gloucestershire Echo*, 6 September 1905; *Dundee Courier*, 21 March 1892.
[2] *Hull Daily Mail*, 17 August 1903.

skills of speaking, writing and organising that enabled them to obtain positions of influence in later life.

Of one Sheffield Chartist, it was said that 'his connection with the movement brought him prominently before the town and paved the way to his entrance at a later date in its municipal and public life'.[3] This was the watchmaker Michael Beal who, with short breaks, served on the town council for twenty two years. The publican George Holloway organised Chartist meetings, sent in reports to the *Star* and collected subscriptions for the Land Company in Kidderminster. Trusting in a man who had shown himself on the side of the people, 'Honest George' was a member of the town council for over forty years. The foreman in a dyeing works in Selkirk, James Brodie served as a town councillor for twelve years. These three men all moved smoothly from Chartism to Liberalism, each helping to establish the Liberal Association in their town. 'I have gone along in one course and have never turned to the right hand or the left', Holloway declared. 'I began as a Liberal and am a Liberal today.'[4]

So across the midlands and the north of England and Scotland in the third quarter of the nineteenth century men who had called themselves Chartists were returned to town councils. It would be impossible to count how many former Chartists were elected councillors, but it would not be unreasonable to estimate the number ran in excess of one hundred. Considerably fewer became ministers. Apart from Charles Clarke, the best example is probably Silas Henn. A Tipton watchmaker Henn was imprisoned with O'Neill in Stafford Gaol after the strikes of 1842. He later became an itinerant Methodist preacher. From the 1850s until the late 1880s this 'intelligent advocate of Christianity' travelled throughout Britain with great success: his sermons were 'very earnest ... pointing out the way in which the sinner may return to his God' and his congregations were 'large and attentive'.[5] For those for whom his sermons were not enough, he also produced tracts such as *Religion in Earnest* (1851) and *Heart's Yearnings* (1859) which enjoyed 'a large circulation'.[6]

[3] *Sheffield Independent*, 7 May 1891.
[4] *Kidderminster Times*, 23 December 1876.
[5] *Irish Times*, 20 July 1859; *Cambridge Independent Press*, 12 November 1864; *Hastings and St. Leonard's Observer*, 1 May 1880.

For George Holloway of Kidderminster, Arthur O'Neill, James Whateley and Charles Clarke were old comrades in the Chartist struggle. He was at O'Neill's graveside in May 1896. When, eight year later Holloway himself died, the inscription on the headstone spoke for all those men who had carried the principles of Chartism into the late nineteenth century: 'Veteran Chartist'.[7]

---

[6] *Gloucestershire Echo*, 19 August 1902.
[7] L.D. Smith, *Carpet Weavers and Carpet Masters: the Hand Loom Carpet Weavers of Kidderminster, 1780-1850* (Kidderminster, 1986), p. 251.

Illustrations

1. Bull Ring Riots, 1839. The Fourth Irish Dragoons advance towards the Bull Ring.

A MODERN ATLAS.

The Postmaster-General is not liable to make good any claim in respect of lost or damaged Parcels."
—*Vide Rules of Inland Parcels Post.*

2. James Whateley campaigned on behalf of the overworked Birmingham postmen.

SEVENTH Year, No. 358. THE DART. Friday, August 31, 1888.

THE "COBDEN" COFFEE HOUSE.

"Let's tak' a cup o' kindness yet."

3. A Chartist teetotaller, James Whateley became a director of the Birmingham Coffee House Company. Here we see William White, chairman of the company, presenting a cup of coffee to Richard Cobden, twenty years dead.

4. The Cobden Hotel in Corporation Street, with 120 bedrooms, opened in May 1885. A temperance hotel, it was built by the Birmingham Coffee House Company at a cost of £20,000. James Whateley ate his breakfast there on the first day it opened.

5. Arthur O'Neill's Zion Baptist Chapel in Newhall Street.

6. George Dixon. In Charles Clarke he found a good friend and a like-minded collaborator in the struggle for working class education.

7. The memorial to George Dawson in Key Hill cemetery, Birmingham. (Photograph by Douglas Wilks).

8. The headstone of James Whateley, now lying flat in Key Hill cemetery, Birmingham. (Photograph by Douglas Wilks).

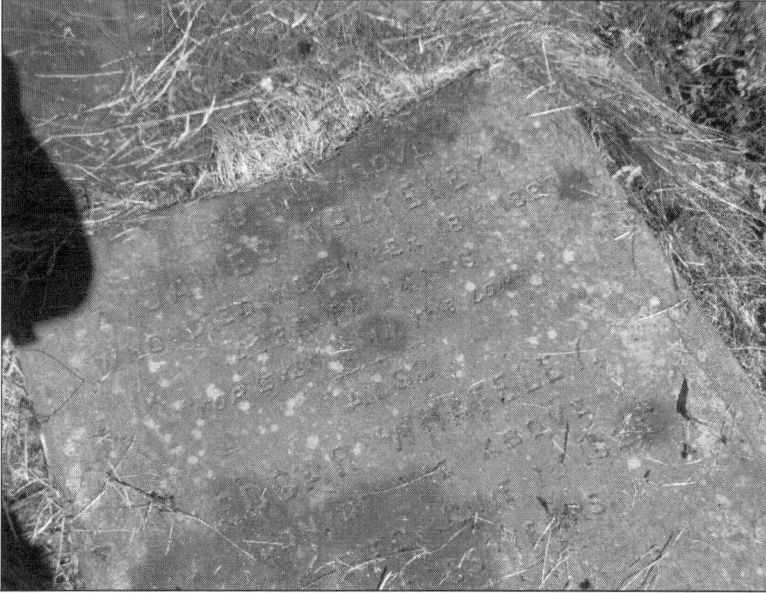

9. Inscription on the headstone of James Whateley. (Photograph by Douglas Wilks).

ST. GEORGE'S CHAMPION.
Councillor James Whateley draws his trusty blade.

10. James Whateley, as seen through the eyes of one of Birmingham's famous satirical magazines. At the time this was published, Whateley represented St. George's ward on the town council.

Index

About the Author

Stephen Roberts is an Honorary Lecturer at the Research School of Humanities and the Arts in the Australian National University and an Honorary Fellow of the Shakespeare Institute in the University of Birmingham. He is the author of nine books and the editor of a further nine, amongst them *The Chartist Prisoners* (2008), *The Parliamentary Career of Charles de Laet Waldo Sibthorp 1826-1855* (2010) and *The Dignity of Chartism: Essays by Dorothy Thompson* (2015).

THE BIRMINGHAM BIOGRAPHIES SERIES

Already published:

Dr J.A. Langford 1823-1903: A Self-Taught Working Man and the Sale of American Degrees in Victorian Britain. 65 pp, 8 photographs, 2014. ISBN: 978 1495475122. £5.99.

Sir Benjamin Stone 1838-1914: Photographer, Traveller and Politician. 102 pp, 20 photographs, 2014. ISBN: 978 1499265521. £7.99.

Mocking Men of Power: Comic Art in Birmingham 1861-1914. 60 cartoons, 2014. ISBN: 978 1502764560. £8.99. (with Roger Ward)

Sir Richard Tangye 1833-1906: A Cornish Entrepreneur in Victorian Birmingham. 65 pp, 2015. ISBN: 978-1512207910. £4.99.

Joseph Chamberlain's Highbury: A Very Public Private House, 44pp, 2015. ISBN: 978-1515044680. £3.99.

Now Mr Editor!: Letters to the Newspapers of Nineteenth Century Birmingham. 100 pp, 2015, ISBN: 978-1518685897. £6.99.

Joseph Gillott: And Four Other Birmingham Manufacturers 1784-1892. 98 pp, 2016. ISBN: 1539483069. £6.99.

Birmingham 1889: One year in a Victorian City. 86 pp. 2017, ISBN 978-1544139227. £4.99.

These books can be ordered from Amazon and other booksellers.

Forthcoming:

Recollections of Victorian Birmingham.

Printed in Great Britain
by Amazon